ANIMALS

THE COLORING BOOK

ALLIGATOR

BEAR

BEARDED DRAGON

BEAVER

BUFFALO

CAMEL

CAT

COBRA

COCKATOO

COW

CRAB

DEER

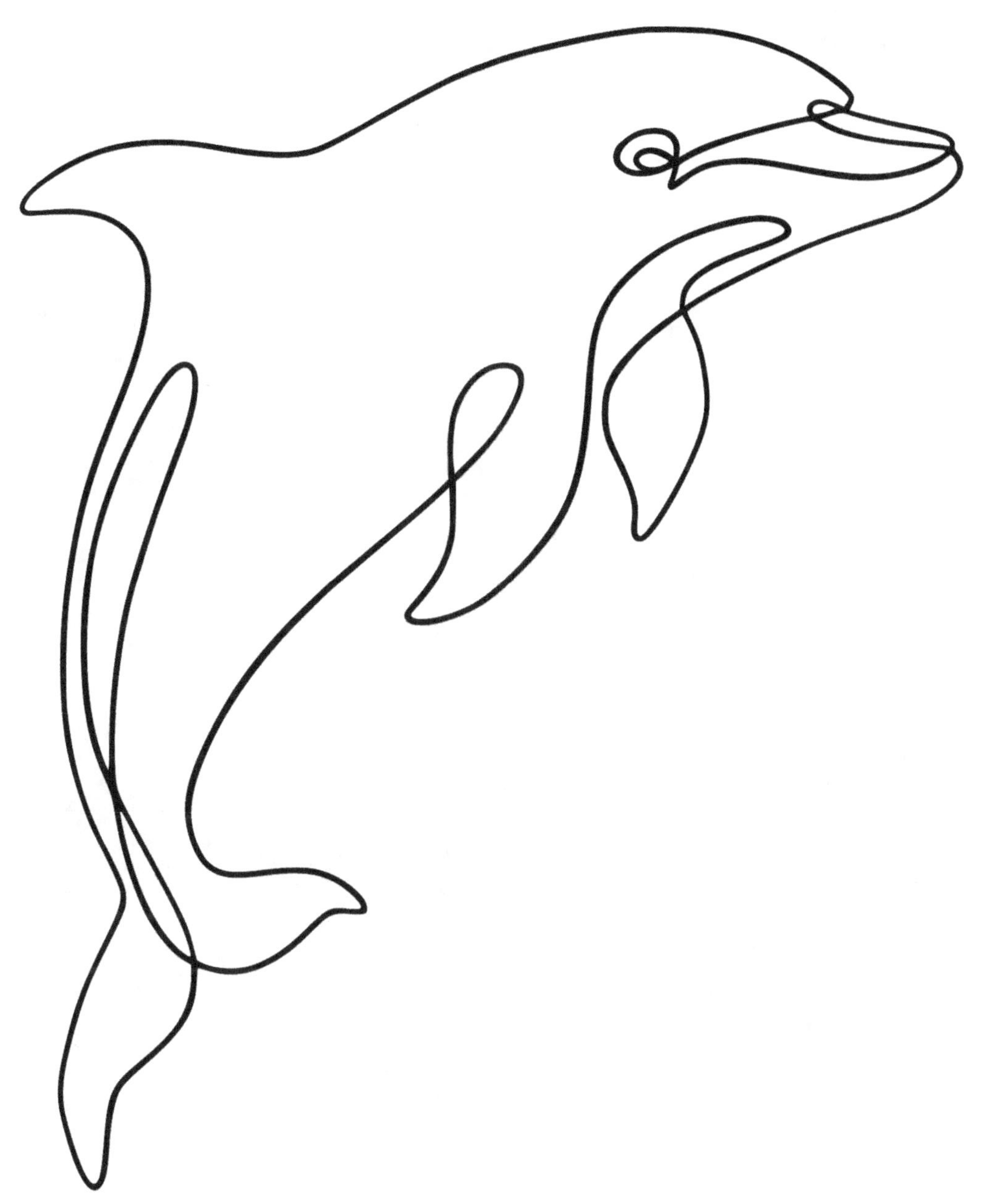

DOLPHIN

DOG

DONKEY

EAGLE

ELEPHANT

FENNEC FOX

FISH

FROG

GIRAFFE

GORILLA

HIPPO

HORSE

HYENA

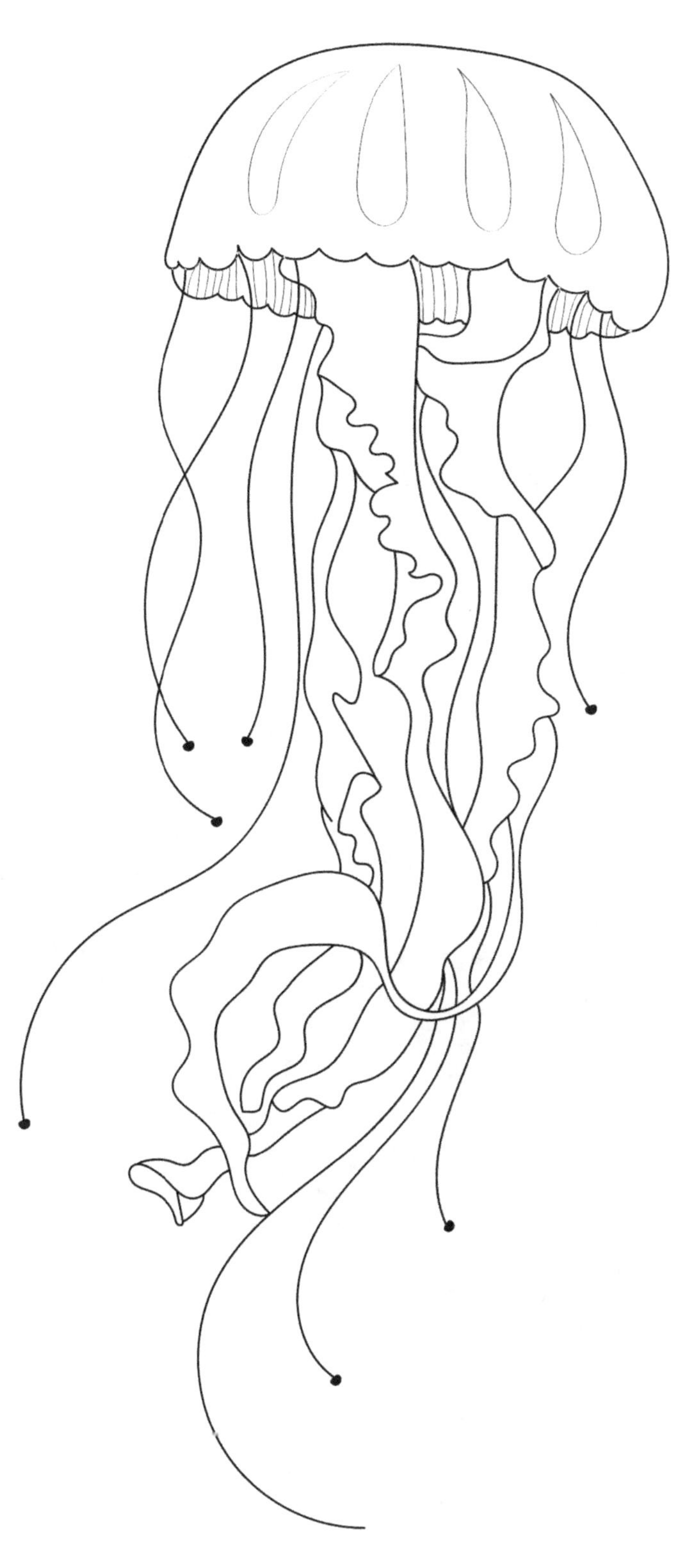

JELLYFISH

KANGAROO

KOALA

LEOPARD

LION

MANATEE

MONKEY

MOOSE

OCTOPUS

OWL

PIG

POLAR BEAR

RHINOCEROS

RIVER OTTER

ROOSTER

SEA OTTER

SEA TURTLE

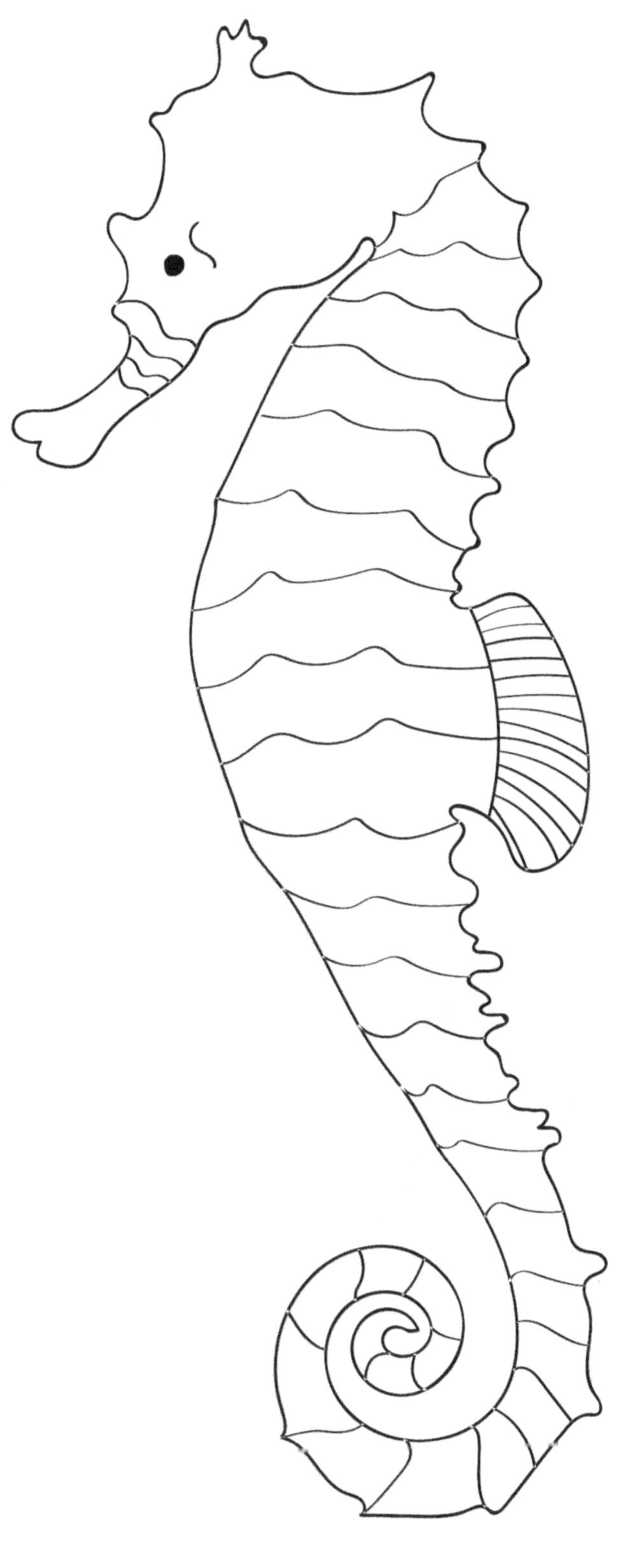

SEAHORSE

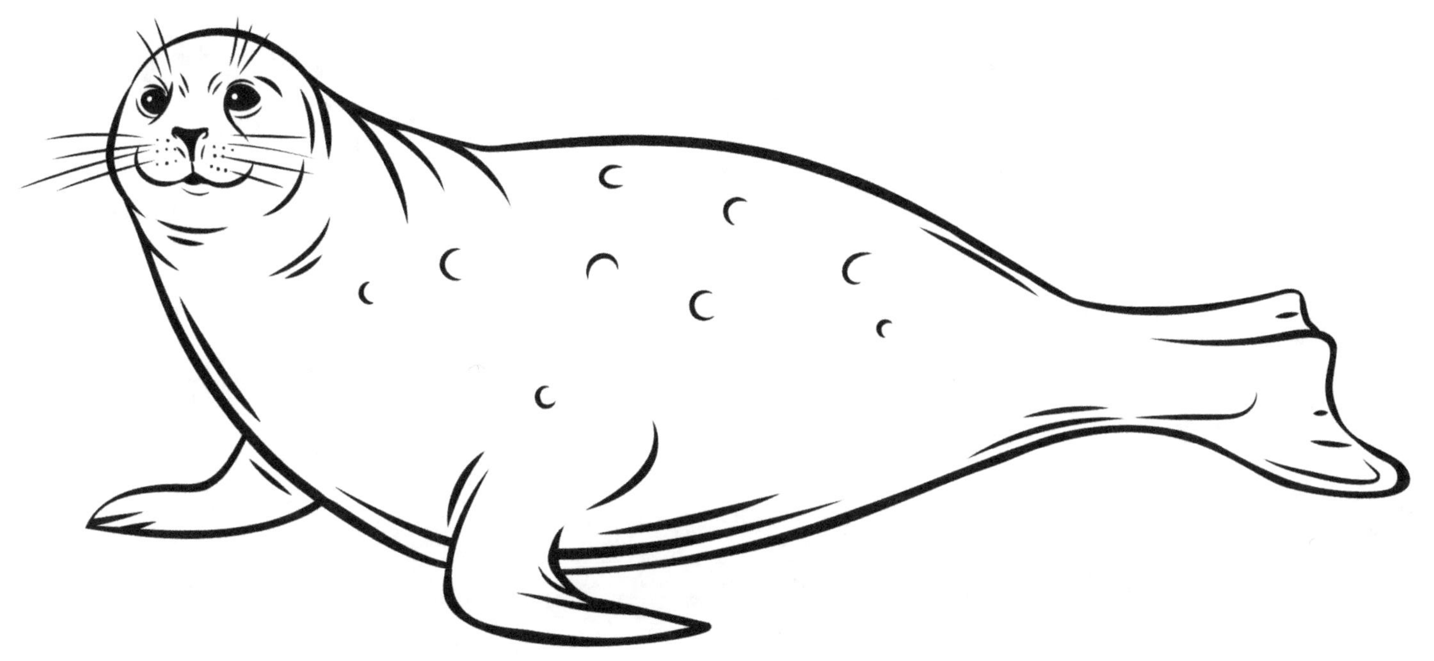

SEAL

SQUIRREL

STARFISH

TIGER

WARTHOG

WOLF

ZEBRA